Donated in memory of
Josephine Gay
12/11/200512/14/2012

Student at Sandy Hook Elementary School
Newtown, Connecticut

Presented by Jean Burke

KODOKU

For Abram—W. E.

To my darling sister, Mariel: with your inspiration
I will never cease to find wonder in the world, with
your companionship I will never be alone. Thank you
for everything.—H. R.

KODOKU

WILLIAM EMERY

Illustrations by Hanae Rivera

Heyday, Berkeley, California

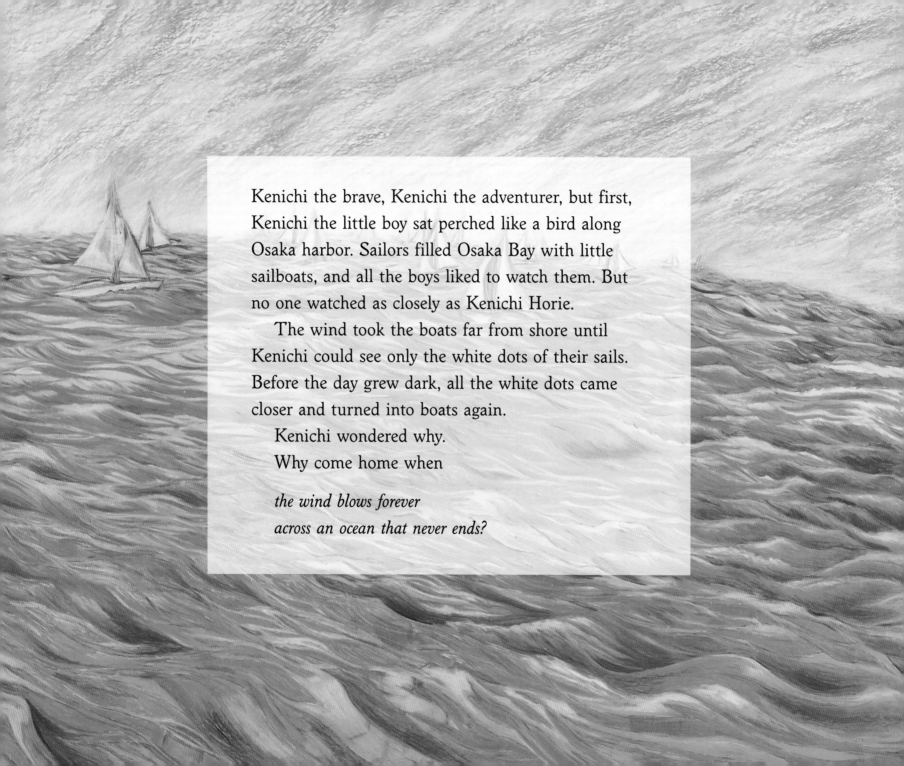

Kenichi the brave, Kenichi the adventurer, but first, Kenichi the little boy sat perched like a bird along Osaka harbor. Sailors filled Osaka Bay with little sailboats, and all the boys liked to watch them. But no one watched as closely as Kenichi Horie.

The wind took the boats far from shore until Kenichi could see only the white dots of their sails. Before the day grew dark, all the white dots came closer and turned into boats again.

Kenichi wondered why.

Why come home when

the wind blows forever
across an ocean that never ends?

Kenichi's journey began with that question. Kenichi began to transform. He studied the living map of the stars. He learned the names of clouds. His hands became practiced with needle and thread.

During the day, Kenichi sailed with men and older boys. They teased him and worked him until his bones ached, but Kenichi never complained. At night, Kenichi drew sailboats, studied them, and then threw the drawings away.

One day, after Kenichi had learned all he could, he visited the shipwright in secret.

"Build this," he said, "but tell no one."

Kenichi visited the shipwright every day after that. Planks were slowly sanded and slowly bent. Wooden mallets slowly drove in wooden pegs. The workers moved so slowly!

"Stop yelling at my workers," said the shipwright. "Your boat will be ready tomorrow."

Finally, the boat Kenichi dreamed was real. It floated proudly before him. He named it: the *Mermaid*.

Kenichi slung a fifty-pound bag of rice over his shoulder. He squeezed rolled maps of the ocean floor and the sky under his arm. He put thirty jars of jam, a radio, and some books into a box and carried it all toward the *Mermaid*. He pulled eighteen gallons of water behind him in a wagon as he walked alone down the deserted streets to the harbor. Shadows filled Osaka Bay. He boarded the *Mermaid*, untied it, and sailed into black Osaka Bay. Only the little old woman who sold rice balls to the sailors saw him go. From Japan to America. From Osaka to San Francisco. From one edge of the Pacific Ocean to the other, because

the wind blows forever
across an ocean that never ends.

But the ocean is a monster, and it is home to monsters. Innocently the *Mermaid* floated, small as an eyelash, across its uncaring surface. The first monster came on cloud feet: the Typhoon!

The ocean scoured the sky. The wind drove its fists into the sea. In between, Kenichi was lost. Helpless. Alone. The typhoon fought the sea for fourteen days before it became bored and went away.

The ocean and the sky were bright and new and calm, but Kenichi could not see them. He sat huddled in a shadow. He had been so scared, but there were no arms to hold him, no eyes to warm him, no voice but his own. He cried out: *Kodoku*— the cry of loneliness. Then Kenichi breathed evenly. He mended the little things the typhoon had broken. A porthole. The sail. His courage.

Swarms of fish followed Kenichi as he sailed. He bent his arm to the water, waited, then snatched the little fish from the sea. The good days tasted like fish.

Sometimes, in the enormity of life, we find friends we will never see again.

Kenichi met a pod of whales sunning themselves lazily in the wide soft ocean. When the wind told him that it was time to leave, he was full of sadness.

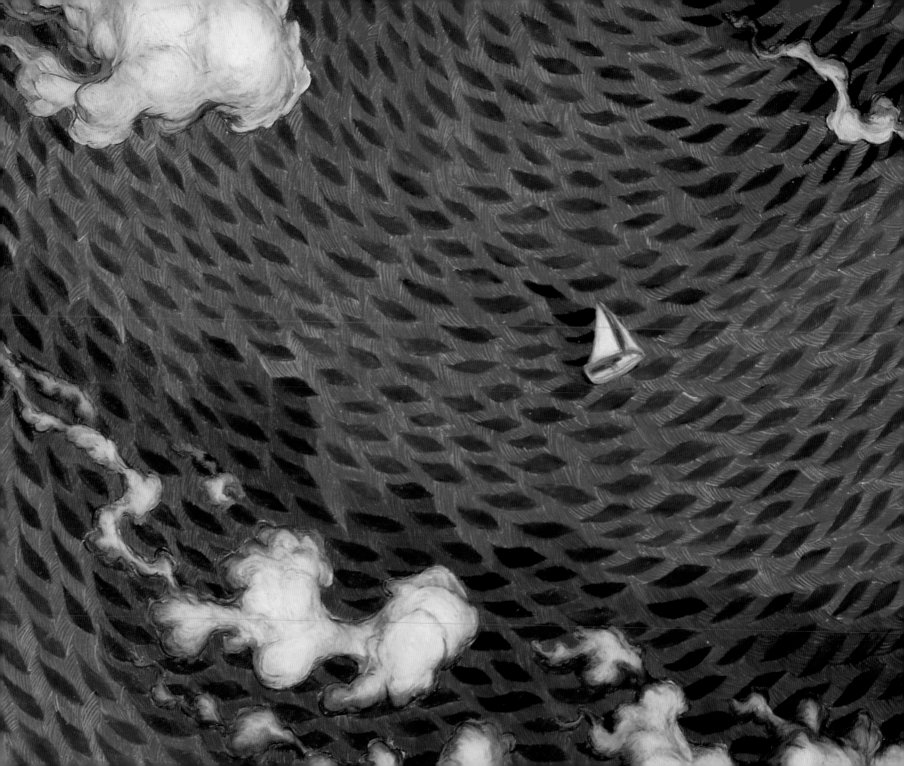

Ships are floating cities propelled across the ocean by enormous engines. They carry thousands of people. They weigh a million pounds. As the *Mermaid* passed through a ship's shadow, Kenichi waved at hundreds of people on deck. Then he sailed on, alone, with only the wind to help him.

The ocean hides great hunters. As the fish liked to follow
Kenichi, sharks liked to follow the fish. When the sharks came to
feed, they slammed against the side of the *Mermaid*. Kenichi hid,
trembling, until they were full, until he was sure they had left.

Kenichi forgot about land. He forgot about everything but the
never-ending ocean, the wind that goes forever. Once the ocean
was full of man-of-wars, jellyfish-like creatures that use the wind
to sail. Kenichi forgot he was not one of them.

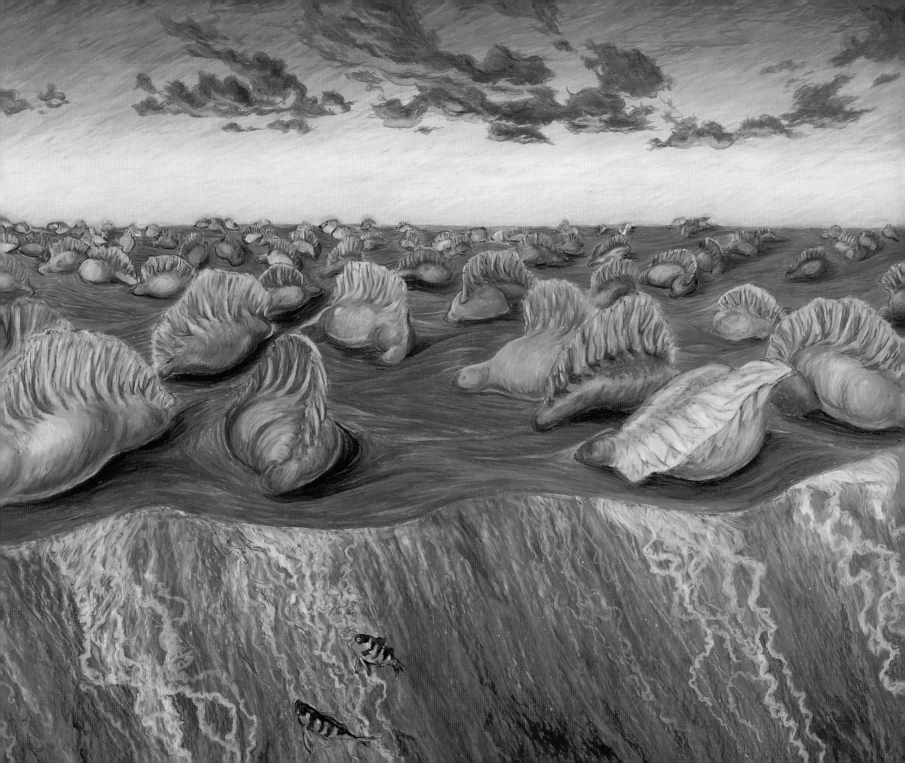

San Francisco carved a hole in the night with its lights. This was the end of his journey. Had he won? Was the ocean defeated? San Francisco Bay is filled with rocks. Biting his lips, Kenichi dropped anchor and waited until morning.

As the sun rose over North America, Kenichi sailed into San Francisco Bay. His soul was as big as a bridge. He stepped onshore and kissed the comforting earth. He burst with joy. But somewhere inside him, he heard, like the beating of a drum, the words:

> *The wind blows forever*
> *across an ocean that never ends.*

Library of Congress Cataloging-in-Publication Data

Justice, William E.
  Kodoku / William Emery ; illustrations by Hanae Rivera.
    p. cm.
  ISBN 978-1-59714-173-4 (hardcover : alk. paper)
  1. Horie, Ken'ichi–Juvenile literature. 2. Mermaid (Boat)–Juvenile literature. 3. Voyages around the world–Juvenile literature. I. Rivera, Hanae. II. Title.
  G440.H798J87 2012
  910.4'1–dc23
                          2011032355

Heyday is an independent, nonprofit publisher and unique cultural institution. We promote widespread awareness and celebration of California's many cultures, landscapes, and boundary-breaking ideas. Through our well-crafted books, public events, and innovative outreach programs we are building a vibrant community of readers, writers, and thinkers. To travel further into California, visit us at www.heydaybooks.com.

Book design by Lorraine Rath

Orders, inquiries, and correspondence should be addressed to:
    Heyday
    P.O. Box 9145, Berkeley, CA 94709
    (510) 549-3564, Fax (510) 549-1889
    www.heydaybooks.com

Printed in China by Everbest Printing Co. through Four Colour Imports, Ltd., Louisville, Kentucky. Printed in October 2012

Job # 111054

10 9 8 7 6 5 4 3 2 1